SOMETIMES I NEED...
HELPING KIDS CARE FOR THEIR HEARTS, MINDS & BODIES

BY GABI GARCIA

ILLUSTRATED BY BIANCA NITA

Sometimes I need movement.
I jump, dance, or run.

I'm squirmy and silly.
It all feels so fun!

Sometimes I need quiet. I'm done. It's too loud.

Sometimes I get grumpy and grouch or talk back.

It may be as simple as needing a snack.

Pizza's a want. Food is a need. I'm always reminded when I start to plead.

I want to stay up. You say I need sleep. Sometimes healthy rules are no fun to keep.

A need is essential. It helps me survive. But beyond food and water, these needs help me thrive.

I need to express myself my own way. I do this all day. I create, build, or play.

I need to contribute, to share, do my part.

No matter how small, helping out fills my heart.

I need to connect and know I belong. To be who I am without feeling wrong.

I need you to love and accept me for me.
When I'm understood, I'm free just to be.

I need to be challenged, to learn and to grow.

I may stumble and fumble then find my own flow.

Sometimes I need help -- I can't do it alone.

But once I have learned, I can go on my own.

I need to feel safe and trust you'll be there, when things are uncertain, too much, or unfair.

I will do my best to let you know what I need.

But when I don't know, I will follow your lead.

Feelings and needs are connected together.
When I understand one, I know them both better.

When I'm happy or proud, a need has been met.

Frustrated or sad? My need's not met yet.

My needs and feelings aren't bad or good.
They're parts of me that can be understood.

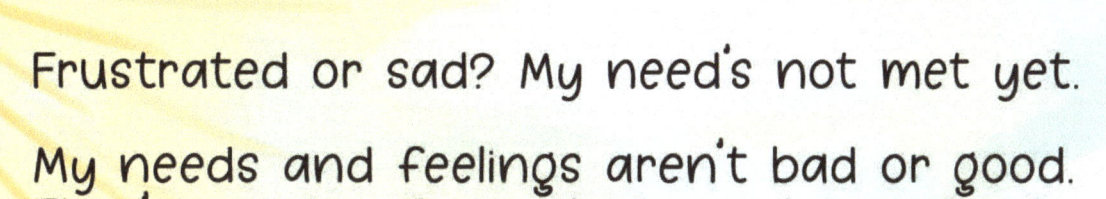

I check in with my body, my heart, and my mind.

Taking care of my needs is loving and kind.

WE ALL HAVE NEEDS

A need is something necessary for people to live a healthy an
happy life.

Physical needs are necessary for you to survive. They also care fc
the well-being of your body. Physical needs include:

ut there are other things you need too. **Emotional needs** are for the well-being of your heart and mind. Here are some motional needs we all have:

LOVE & BELONGING
Having respectful and supportive relationships with yourself and others. Being understood, valued, and accepted as you are.

SELF-EXPRESSION
Sharing your thoughts, feelings, and ideas. Using creativity, curiosity, and imagination to be you!

SIGNIFICANCE
Knowing you matter and can make a difference.

PLAY & LEARNING
Doing things you enjoy. Working through challenges on your own.

NEEDS & FEELINGS

Your feelings and needs go together.

These are some feelings you may notice when your needs are not met:

- confused
- cranky
- disappointed
- embarrassed
- frustrated
- hurt
- lonely
- sad
- tired
- worried

These are some feelings you may notice when your needs are met:

- amazed
- confident
- content
- enthusiastic
- friendly
- hopeful
- peaceful
- proud
- rested
- thankful

→ Practice making the connection between your feelings and needs.

I feel _____ because I need _____.

When my need for _____ is met, I feel _____.

**Needs and feelings aren't good or bad.
They're parts of you that you can learn to pay attention to.**

CHECK-IN WITH YOUR BODY, HEART, & MIND

Pause.

Take a deep breath.

What do you need? ♥

Sometimes, just knowing what you need is helpful.

Other times, it's necessary to let someone know so they can help you get your needs met.

A NOTE TO CAREGIVERS:

To the caring adult who chose this book, thank you! It's as much for you as it is for the child you're reading this to. That's because your child needs supportive, loving adults to help meet their physical and emotional needs. When this is done consistently, they thrive!

In addition to having their basic physical needs met, children need us to be attuned to them. They need us to listen, be empathic, and provide a sense of safety and belonging for them in the world. They need us to play and explore with them, trust their capabilities, provide predictable routines, and set boundaries. In short, they need care for their hearts, minds, and bodies.

I hope this book will provide a springboard for you and your child to explore and better understand the needs we all share yet rarely talk about. To be human is to have needs, and helping your child understand and communicate theirs is a gift.

One essential understanding from this book is that needs and feelings are connected. When our needs aren't met, difficult emotions arise. Needs and feelings aren't good or bad. They're parts of us we need to pay attention to.

When you're able to understand (and help your child understand) that the challenging feelings they experience signal an unmet need, you're more likely to respond with empathy, curiosity, and compassion. Modeling this teaches your child that having those needs and feelings is okay.

Once the need or feeling has been identified, you can help your child find ways to meet those needs. Helping your child become more mindful of what their heart, mind, and body needs is empowering! As they learn to identify and express their needs, they get to know and understand themselves more deeply.

Warmly,
Gabi

Hi, I'm Gabi.

Thank you for choosing this book. I'm a mama, children's book author, and licensed professional counselor. I spent 21 years learning from the children I worked with in the public schools, something I am immensely grateful for. These experiences, along with just being a human on this planet, inspire the books I write.

I believe in the power and beauty of books. I hope that the ones I write will be of service to parents, educators, and other caregivers, and of course children, and contribute in some small way toward making this world a better place. You can find out more on my website: gabigarciabooks.com.

If you found this book useful, I would sincerely appreciate your honest review! It's one of the best ways to help others find it.

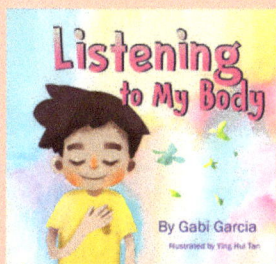
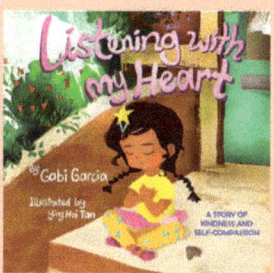
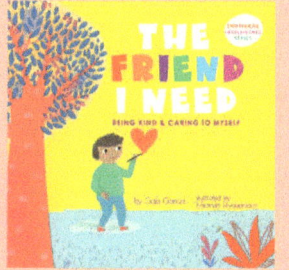
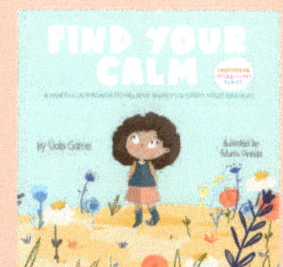

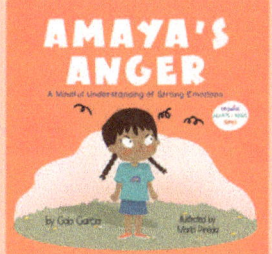
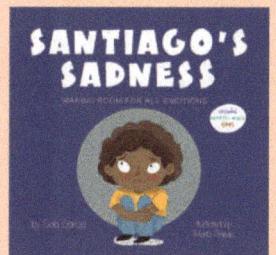
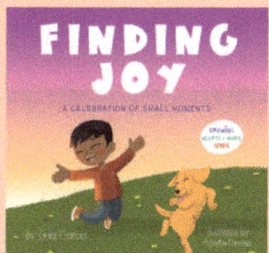
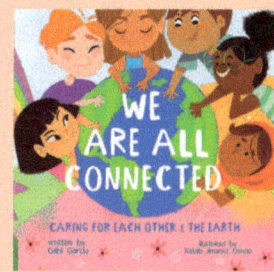
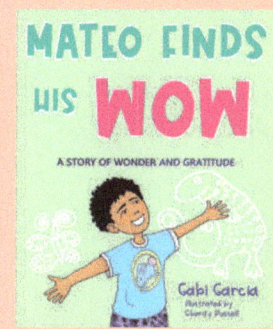

ALL TITLES AVAILABLE IN SPANISH

Hi, I'm Bianca.

I'm a children's illustrator with a passion for creating playful and imaginative art for meaningful projects. Born in Romania, I now travel the world, infusing the best inspiration into my work from the places I visit. I'm a self-taught artist and believe that everyone can become and have everything they wish for if they believe in themselves and constantly work on their dreams.

When not illustrating, you might find me playing sports, hiking, going on nature walks, reading, singing, dancing, or trying out some delicious food.

You can follow my journey @biancanitaillustration (on Instagram). 😊

For my daughter, Liliana, and for all children:
You matter. May you always know the specialness of who you are.

Copyright © 2023 by
Gabi Garcia Books, LLC
gabigarciabooks.com
Illustrations by Bianca Nita

902 Gardner Road no. 4
Austin, Texas 78721

skinned knee publishing

Identifiers: ISBN: 978-1-949633-66-5 (hardcover) | 978-1-949633-67-2 (paperback) | 978-1949633-68-9(ebook)

The information in this book is not intended to be used, no should it be used, to diagnose or treat any mental health or medical condition. For diagnosis or treatment or any mental health or medical condition, consult a licensed professional, psychologist or physician. The publisher and author are not responsible or liable for any damages or negative consequences from any treatment, action, application or preparation to any person reading or following the information in this book.

www.ingramcontent.com/pod-product-compliance
Lightning Source LLC
Chambersburg PA
CBHW041231240426
43673CB00010B/304